The Kabbalah of Masonry & Related Writings

By

William Wynn Westcott, Eliphas Levi,
Leopold F. Strauss & J. Ralston Skinner

Copyright © 2020 Lamp of Trismegistus. All rights reserved. No part of this publication may be reproduced or transmitted in any form or by any means, electronic or mechanical, including photocopying, recording, or by any information storage and retrieval system, without permission in writing from Lamp of Trismegistus. Reviewers may quote brief passages.

ISBN: 978-1-63118-453-6

Foundations of Freemasonry Series

Other Books in this Series and Related Titles

The Mysteries of Freemasonry & the Druids
by Albert G. Mackey, Manly P. Hall, &c (978-1-63118-444-4)

Royal Arch, Capitular and Cryptic Masonry
by various authors (978-1-63118-425-3)

Masonic Symbolism of Easter and the Christ in Masonry
by various authors (978-1-63118-434-5)

The Two Great Pillars of Boaz and Jachin
by Albert G. Mackey &c (978-1-63118-433-8)

Masonic Symbolism of King Solomon's Temple
by Albert G. Mackey &c (978-1-63118-442-0)

The Regius Poem or Halliwell Manuscript
by King Solomon (978-1-63118-447-5)

Masonic Life of George Washington
by Albert G. Mackey (978-1-63118-457-4)

The Lost Keys of Freemasonry or The Secret of Hiram Abiff
by Manly P. Hall (978-1-63118-427-7)

Masonic Symbolism of the Apron & the Altar
by various authors (978-1-63118-428-4)

Symbolism and Discourses on the Entered Apprentice, Fellowcraft and Master Mason Blue Lodge Degrees by various (978-1-63118-413-0)

The Story and Legend of Hiram Abiff by William Harvey, Manly P. Hall & Albert G. Mackey (978-1-63118-411-6)

Symbolism of the Corner Stone, the North East Corner and the Religious & Masonic Symbolism of Stones by various (978-1-63118-412-3)

Audio Versions are also Available on Audible and iTunes

Table of Contents

Introduction...7

The Kabbalah of Masonry
by William Wynn Westcott...9

Gematria and the Letter G
by Leopold F. Strauss ...23

Kabbalah and the Origin of Freemasonry
by Eliphas Levi...37

Notes on the Kabbalah of the Old Testament
by J. Ralston Skinner...45

Introduction

From the beginning of Modern Freemasonry's birthdate of 1717, the intelligentsia of humanity have found refuge for safe reflection within the walls of the fraternity. Masonic writers have produced a nearly incalculable amount of written musings on a multitude of esoteric and philosophical subjects, as they relate to the ancient mysteries that Freemasonry currently storehouses. Sadly, most of it appears to have sat largely unread, as American Freemasonry in particular, continues to transform itself into something that bears little resemblance to what it was originally designed to be. The true essence of Freemasonry is not that of blind patriotism or a single-minded national religion but one of Universal Brotherhood and altruism, designed for the betterment not just of its members but of society as a whole. In particular, for those who are not members of the fraternity, as Freemasonry has always acted as a beacon, to help guide humanity through darker times, with the hopes that one day we will collectively reach a truly enlightened age.

It's not uncommon for new members joining the fraternity to find little education within the walls of many modern lodges, in spite of so much written material available to the membership. Many older members are not simply uneducated with regards to real Masonic history and symbology, not to mention the vast arena of related subjects, but they are disinterested in all of it, as well.

Lamp of Trismegistus is doing its part to help preserve humanity's Masonic history by making some of these classics available to those students who are seeking to unearth the knowledge of these ancient colossi. As such, Lamp of Trismegistus offers its readers highlights of Masonic study, culled from a variety of authors and viewpoints, with the hope bringing education back into the fraternity. So, be sure to check out other titles in our *Foundations of Freemasonry Series* as well as our *Esoteric Classics, Theosophical Classics, Occult Fiction, Paranormal Classics, Supernatural Fiction* and our *Christian Apocrypha Series*, and don't be afraid to let a little altruism into your own heart or even into your Lodge. You can also download the audio versions of most of these titles from iTunes or Audible, for learning on the go.

The Kabbalah of Masonry
By William Wynn Westcott

Freemasonry, our English Craft, describes itself as a "system of morality veiled in allegory, and illustrated by symbols." A little consideration will, I feel sure, convince us that it is something more than this.

'Tis not the whole of life to live, Nor all of death to die,'

wrote the poet Montgomery, and the aphorism is applicable also to Freemasonry.

Our Ritual presents us with ample internal evidence that the mystery of the Craft lies deeper than a mere scheme of moral maxims. Our Ritual contains distinct prayers, addressed to the clearly defined one God; the Unity of the God we address is the essence of his type.

Our Ritual includes several most serious obligations. To what? To morality? No, to secrecy. These obligations are taken subject to certain penalties. What penalties? Fine? Or seclusion? No, to penalties of whose nature we are all aware and which I need not therefore particularize.

Can any rational man believe that such formulae were originally designed for the purpose of veiling a scheme of morality; a system of morals suitable to all men, whose realization would be the achievement of earthly perfection? Our Ritual embodies and traces out a definite legend, or set of legends, it insists on the acceptance of these events as positive truth, wholly apart from any evidence from common history. Nay, even in spite of it. These events must be grasped by the perfect mason as masonic truth, and not believed only, but personally acted. Could such an unusual, not to say unnatural, claim on a man be made simply to veil a moral precept? Could such a state of mind and body be made peremptory simply to paint a beautiful allegory?

Our mysteries are positively guarded by signs, tokens, and words, so stringently accorded and so carefully preserved, the profane are clearly convinced that even the most apparently reliable exposés of them are but make-believes. If these secret modes of recognizable shrouded but a scheme to make men more honest, or more charitable, is it reasonable to suppose that this sanctity would have grown up around them?

No, my brethren, it would have been but a vain and foolish association which should have been created to make a secret of morality.

Freemasonry, then, must be something more, much more. To us, the representatives of the Freemasonry of today it may be but a light thing, and I fear it often is. But let us remember our great claim, the early original of our Order, there must be our hunting ground for the cause of our secrecy, for the constitution of the Fraternity, for the intense obligations imposed on each one of us.

And now I should ask each of you what is the greatest aim of an earthly existence? Is it not to prepare for another? Do we not all feel assured that, we must come to an end of this terrene existence? Do we not feel that the "I," the "Ego" within each one of us cannot end with this world? *"To sleep, to die, perchance to dream; ay, there's the rub."*

The aim of each mortal, then, is to grasp at an ideal life, to prepare for another stage of existence; and how? How but through one's Creator? Who else could make or mar my life-but I and my Creator? Religion is the name we mortals give to our aspirations towards our Creator, and to our schemes to read Him.

Religion, then, is the key to try in this secret lock; a secret religion might need hiding, what from? Whom from? From one's Creator? No; from one's fellow man, who in time past as far as history can reach, has never failed to sully the face of this fair earth with blasphemies, with idolatry, with persecutions, with religious martyrdom. Religious zeal and intolerance have been too often but convertible terms.

To combat the risk of death what weapon should we expect to find chosen? What but, the threat of death? Not a perfect weapon possibly, not an ideally perfect one, not a heavenly one; but one applicable and competent to protect against evil doers.

Now Freemasonry has, it has appeared, a grand central

idea, a creator, a One God. Does history give us any record that the holders of such a dogma have been the mass of the inhabitants, or the greatest men throughout the world, or throughout the centuries? Or does history show us that believers in a unique impersonal Deity, pure and undefiled, not consenting unto iniquity, have ever been aught but a minority, often persecuted, and always reviled? The minority has doubtless been a growing one, and has of late been too important to be crushed by threats of death, and in a parallel mode we now find as I pointed out at first we have even arrived at the stage of having forgotten why our obligations were designed.

Such, my brethren, is the suggestion of my theme; our present system of allegorical morality is the lineal descendant of true veiled Monotheism, which in a pagan and persecuting world had need in every clime and in every age of some scheme of self-defense.

We may not be able to trace in definite order every step in the vast procession of forms through which the Monotheistic secret has been shrouded, veiled, and preserved, or even to trace a distinct groove in the wheel of time in any one nation or century, but history is at no time free from the survival of scraps of evidence that a mystic association was at work, preserving and consecrating some high ideal, some great dogma.

The absence of distinct and definite histories of secret Monotheistic societies is really an evidence of their reality and of their successful operation, and the vast number of forms assumed by the true Believers, at one time resembling a military organization, at another a priesthood, at another a philosophic sect, at another time the secret held by three, two, or even one man—a king—at others of wide-spread significance, is to me but evidence of the reality of my contention.

And I affirm, and could afford considerable evidence in support of the view that even among the priesthood of what have apparently been the most debased and extravagant religions, there has always existed an esoteric doctrine held by a select hierarchy, and that doctrine the Unity of God, as a Creator, Designer, and Ruler, apart from the modes of His manifestation to us mortals, whether by processes and sublime emanations, or by Sonship, or by influence of the Holy Spirit, or by the development in sex, or by maternity; all of these modes of representing the action of a unique impersonal God, in relation to His works.

The Jews have ever been true Monotheists and have been ever persecuted, and the Old Testament, their own narrative of themselves, is perhaps the chief extant volume recording struggles to preserve a pure Theocracy, to preserve a religion of Monotheism, pure and free from idolatry. And although at times we find, superficially speaking, the whole Jewish nation gone astray, yet there is collateral evidence that there were at every epoch some true believers.

As the Jewish power declined, and at length fell, pure Monotheism trembled, and had to shroud its head for a long period from the dominant pagan conqueror. Hence arose one series of secret associations which has extended down to our own times, and whose development is now in our midst as Freemasonry, to me the lineal descendant of the early schemes and associations designed to perpetuate a pure religion and a corresponding system of moral ethics.

Our secret brotherhood, note, has a specially Judaic basis, our main legend is connected with that greatest Jewish law giver and ruler, Solomon. Our present doctrine is a Trinitarianism, clothed with the Christian virtues. If Freemasonry arose as an entirely new scheme in the 16th or 17th century it must have arisen in a Christian land, and would certainly have been marked by specially Trinitarian features, which would have remained permanent.

Now as collateral evidence of my contention I pray you to follow me into the consideration that in our Freemasonry may yet be traced allusions and references to that system of esoteric teaching and dogma, which was undeniably the result of the destruction of the exoteric Monotheism of Judea, I mean the Jewish Kabbalah which first took shape as a definite secret Sophia, wisdom or doctrine after the Fall of Jerusalem, and which was founded on the basis of the Monotheistic truths accumulated during centuries of more or less pure outward observance of a Monotheistic religion.

This Kabbalah then crystallized gradually into a theological scheme, and became more and more elaborated through the dark-ages following the ruin of the Augustan era;

to dominant paganism followed utter ignorance of the masses until a dawn arose in Europe and a Monotheism was developed anew, not Jewish, but Christian, and became exoteric, and its exotericism became its weakness, and its priesthood became once more self-seeking, and neglected the primal truth-yet even through this period the esoteric purity was preserved by the few, by the learned, by the pious.

I will not wander into the area of discussion which rages around the sole origin of Freemasonry from trade guilds, from Templarism, from the Jewish race, from the Hermeticists, or from the Rosicrucians.

I am content to recognize that all these associations have been concerned in its growth, and am content that our present system points only to the cardinal truth, confessing that in its progression along the ladder of time it has been assisted by each and all of these, and has survived them, and has thus proved its right to exist. To say the least of it, the mystery would only be increased by a dogma that the officials of Freemasonry in the seventeenth century were so intensely learned that they constructed proprio motu, such a system, in which the doctrines and essays of the most ancient Aporreta shine forth.

The Kabbalah as a system of Theosophy has pre-eminent claims to be considered *primus inter pares*, among all the theistic speculations of mankind, which have a bearing on, and have taken part in the formation of, the Masonic Aphanism. I shall briefly point out a few masonic points which are illuminated by a comparison with the Kabbalah. Some references to the mysteries are conveniently interspersed, of these there is much evidence that the Egyptian forms are the oldest; now it must be specially remembered that the Lecture on the Tracing Board of the first degree actually refers to these customs of the ancient Egyptians as the fount of origin for many masonic points; it refers also to the doctrines of Pythagoras whose five pointed star I mention later on.

Among the masonic points, which have been derived from the ancient mysteries, I notice the triple degrees of the system, corresponding to the mysteries of Serapis, Iris, and Osiris. Now our second degree has feminine suggestions; note, Shibboleth, the ear of corn, the water, for corn refers to the goddess Ceres, female, or Demeter, Gemeter, earth mother, and water is female in all old languages; compare Binah, mother deity; and our third is a very close approximation to that which represented the slaying of Osiris. The battery of acclamation when the candidate is restored to light is a direct imitation of the sudden clash of feigned thunder and lightning by which the neophyte of the Eleusinian mysteries was greeted. The death of Osiris and resurrection as Horus are represented as the decease of the fellow craft and the raising of a new master mason.

The entered apprentice is referred to three lights, these are Osiris in the east, Isis in the west, and Horus who was master or living lord in place of Osiris, in the south. Note also that there is no light in the north, the type of night and of darkness, in this also the idea is an ancient one. The three great, though emblematic lights compose a bright triangle, the three lesser lights an inferior or darker one, the two combined may be considered in a group as a six-pointed star, the Hexapla, or Seal of Solomon, which was also a notable emblem in all the old initiations. The Hexapla was a type of the number six, esteemed a male number assigned by the Kabbalists to Microprosopus, the *Vau* of the Hebrew alphabet, and of the Tetragrammaton, the six middle Sephiroth, especially the median 6th, the Tiphereth, or Beauty of the Deity.

The Pentalpha, or emblem of health, the Pythagorean emblem, is the five-pointed Masonic star, five in the Hebrew *He*, a female potency according to the Kabbalah, and may be either the superior *He*, the mother idea, or the lower *He*, the Bride of God, the Church. The Kingdom, the two together constitute the Elohim, a feminine plural noun, constantly used as a title for creative power in the narrative of Genesis in chapter one, and up to the end of verse four of chapter two, where the Jehovist narrative commences.

It is a curious coincidence that the Acacia referring to the burial of Hiram Abiff, and which the fellowcrafts, dressed in white, carried in their hands as emblems of their innocence, is the same word as the Greek ἀκακία, which means innocence; it was also an emblem of mortality.

The insistence on a candidate for masonry proving himself free from deformity is a requirement which was common to the selection from among the Levites of a priest of the Jews (see Leviticus xxi., 18), and to the reception of a neophyte in both the Egyptian and the Eleusinian mysteries, and a further point of resemblance is seen in the refusal to admit a slave, or any but a free man. If the whole aim of Freemasonry were to propagate brotherly love and charity, why refuse to extend its blessings to the cripple, or the maimed, or to him in subjection.

The legend of the Three Grand Masters, of whom one is lost—becomes removed to the invisible world—is a curious image of the Kabbalistic first triad of the emanations of the unseen and unknowable Ain Soph Aur, the boundless one, boundless light, first is Kether the Crown, thence proceed Chochmah and Binah, wisdom and understanding, and then is the Crown concealed and lost to perception in its exaltedness, the word is lost and replaced by other titles.

In the Ten Sephiroth, as in our Lodges, we are taught of two great pillars, one on the right and on the left, the pillars of Mercy and Judgment; then a third exists between them, that of severity, tempered by mercy, and called pillar of Mildness. These are similar to the Masonic pillars of Wisdom, Strength and Beauty, while the Ain Soph Aur above them is the Mystic Blazing Star in the East. Wisdom Strength and Beauty are the Sephirotic Triad of Chochmah, Geburah, and Tiphereth.

The several emanations of the Sephiroth of the Kabbalah, one proceeding from the other, produce, as they are always designed in visible form, a tortuous path, at once reminding us of the Winding Staircase. Indeed one form of the contemplation of the Eternal was described by the Kabbalists as ascending by the Sephirotic names and descending by the paths. This tortuous path is also like the lightning flash, as is said in the "Sepher Yetzirah" or "Book of Formations," which has been translated by myself, and is, perhaps, the oldest monotheistic philosophical tract in existence. Note, the Son of God is also spoken of as the "Light of the World."

Four tassels refer to four cardinal virtues, says the first degree Tracing Board Lecture, these are temperance, fortitude, prudence, and justice; these again were originally branches of the Sephirotic Tree, Chesed first, Netzah fortitude, Binah prudence, and Geburah justice. Virtue, honor, and mercy, another triad, are Chochmah, Hod, and Chesed.

Another well-known Sephiroth Triad deserves mention here, the concluding phrase of the Lord's Prayer, of the Prayer Book version, which, however, is not found in the Douay version, nor in the revised New Testament, viz: the kingdom, the power, and the glory—Malkuth, Netzah, and Hod.

As may be seen by the diagram many triads may be formed, and different authors speak of different numbers; thus Frater S. C. Gould, of Manchester, New Hampshire, describes nine; Fra. MacGregor Mathers notes ten but even more may be formed, of course, if relative sequence be not insisted upon.

The Winding Staircase consisted of 3, 5 and 7 steps, if not of more, of these, three referred to the three Rulers of a Lodge, these are the three mother letters of the Hebrew alphabet, *Aleph, Mem, Shin*, typical again of fire, air, and water, the three first Sephiroth. Five to hold a Lodge and seven to make it perfect, these are the Hebrew seven double letters, parallel emblems to seven planets and seven lower Sephiroth. Three, five and seven amount to fifteen, which is equivalent to JAH, God, *Yod*, and *He*, ten and five; every Hebrew word is also a number, and the reverse. These seven persons, again, are typical of the seven most learned Rabbis who held the Assembly named in the Zohar, Idra Suta, in which the essence of Deity is discussed as a Holy Mystery. The still more Holy Assembly of Rabbis, the Idra Rabba included three more, these formed the Keepers of the Veils of the original Royal Arch Chapter, for whom the lower offices of Treasurer, Inner Guard and Sentinel are now substituted; some very learned patron of the order caused this change to be made, fearing that it might be a blasphemy to represent these three highest powers in a Lodge which might become too ordinary a business. They were types of the first Sephirotic Triad. Freemasons little know how close they have been to the personation of the most exalted types of Omnipotence.

The letter G in the center of a Fellowcrafts' Lodge, has received several explanations; I would add that it has a relation to *Gimel*, the Hebrew G, the third letter of the alphabet, the three, meaning Trinity of Deity; the third Sephira is Binah, the mother of Microprosopus, the son, a feminine potency, Mother of God, with uncial Greek capital G. The present masonic interpretation is folly, the idea of a modern ornamental lecturer.

Again the two parallel lines, the one Moses, the other King Solomon, enclosing a circle, bearing a central point, is entirely Kabbalistic. The point is Tiphereth, beauty of conduct within a circle of virtues and bounded by the pillars Mercy and

Justice.

Regard for a moment the varying titles; Great Architect, the Foundation, Yesod the center of the lowest triad.

Grand Geometrician, the beauty of design, Tiphereth, center of the median triad.

Most High, the awful Kether, the Crown, partly concealed, at sight of whose face a mortal, unprepared, must die. Notice the grandeur and mystery increases as we pass up the Masonic ladder or the Sephirotic Tree.

The perambulation by the candidate under appropriate guidance is an apt imitation of the ceremony in the Ancient Mysteries.

Another remnant of the same form was until recently, and may be still, extant in Scotland, the highland custom Deasil was to walk three times round a person in the direction of the sun, for favorable effect. To perambulate against the sun was called Widdershins, and was an evil omen and act.

Freemasonry, as one special development of a long series of Monotheistic secret associations, being constituted on a basis of masonic operations by masculine operatives, has perhaps necessarily excluded females; many military and hierarchical mystical societies have also from their essence consisted of males alone. The very low state of female culture in the ancient world and during the middle ages, also no doubt contributed towards the exclusion of women from mystic rites and from active interference with religions ceremonies; an exclusion which, were we about to constitute a new form of concealed worship, would hardly be tolerated in the present year of grace, and certainly could not be defended in argument. This ancient exclusion of women from secret rites (*to which there were a few exceptions*) has been expanded also in another direction, with baneful result: I refer to the complete removal of all female types, forms, and stages from the ideas of the higher powers, angels, archangels, and the emanations of Deity, which certainly existed in the oldest forms of the Kabbalah, and in the minds of the composers of the early chapters of the Pentateuch. It cannot be doubted that a very large number of minds cling firmly to the Roman Catholic type of religion, owing to its insistence of reverence and praise to the beatified woman—Mary—who is representative of the ancient views of the female counterpart of God-head.

With this digression I must conclude, and I beg for a lenient judgment on these discursive remarks on our mystic order, for even if the views be erroneous, they may yet call up a refutation which shall be found of great value to the brethren present, and Freemasons in general.

Gematria and the Letter G

By Leopold F. Strauss

In every Masonic lodge room there is presented for special notice, exhibited for particular consideration, the letter G. At all Masonic expositions, shows or manifestations, on Masonry's golden or gilded emblems, on all the so very varied Masonic symbolic configuration, we find embedded, and as it were enshrined, this letter G. On special occasions, feasts and celebrations, this letter looks with glowing radiance upon the assembly of Free and Accepted Masons.

Now the question arises, or rather should arise, what is the significance of this letter G, that it should be given such an all-surpassing prominence in the Masonic realm? What was the idea or ideas, what was the object, the purpose of the pioneers, the founders of Modern Freemasonry in giving such an illustrious position to this character or symbol?

This emblematic G is a cogent illustration of the phenomenon that the large majority of human beings wandering upon this planet Earth, spend their lives and finally complete their destined pilgrimage, without ever troubling themselves as to the goal, or the purposes of Providence or God. The *raison d'etre* of things, of the world, does not take up much of their attention. They spend little of their valuable time in wondering about the things, which they feel, smell, taste, hear or see. The would-be teacher or monitor is told in irritated voice: "What difference does it make?" In other words, "What can I buy for it?" The how, where, why and when, gives no trouble to the average good American, German, or French citizen.

Now this letter G is too conspicuous, too prominent, to be left altogether out of consideration by the honorable "Guides of the Worthy Members of Modern Freemasonry." So in one carefully arranged scene, at a definitely appointed time, the Guide gives the Candidate a brief elucidation of this so conspicuous, so omnipresent figure. In reverential voice, with solemn mien, the Candidate is informed that the letter G has a double meaning; that being the first letter of the two words, it represents two ideas: the measurable material, and the incalculable spiritual and divine. The Guide, of course, simply repeats the memorized phrases, the words he himself was told when he was a Candidate.

A little reflection should bring this consideration: the letter G is the initial letter for the word God in the English and Germanic languages only. Yet, it is as conspicuous, as omnipresent, in the Italian, French, Spanish, Slavic and Albanian lodge rooms as in the English American-Germanic lodges. The initial letter of the word for God in the so-called Romance languages, Latin, French and Italian, is D; in Slavic languages B and in the Albanian language is P. Why then in these countries is this letter G not changed into D, B or P?

Again, geometry is only a small part, a short section of the great domain called mathematics. The school child has his troubles with arithmetic; the student has his or her difficulties with algebra, trigonometry, calculus, etc. Why enthrone geometry for this special consideration, meditation and reverence? *"The hardest thing in the world is to think,"* says Emerson.

In this connection we will add this: the Candidate sees, in the course of his Masonic career, some strange things, some very remarkable scenes and sceneries; he hears some strange words and phrases in the memorized proclamations of the Masters, the Chiefs and the High Priests. But the large majority of the honorable members of Modern Freemasonry are in the same mental condition, or enlightenment, about Freemasonry as would be a well-trained, docile, puppy or kitten on the subject of art, when puppy or kitten is carried through a most munificent palace or art museum. Its eyes might be directed and steadily turned toward some special, highly valued paintings or pieces of sculpture, and yet our patient kitten or puppy, much like a member of the Free and Accepted Masons, will not ask a single question, will not even wonder, no matter what is placed before its healthy, innocent eyes.

Now let us return to our letter G. What is this letter G?

It is for one thing, the initial letter of the word Gematria. But what is Gematria? The word itself constitutes a kind of combination of two others, of the two words Grammateia and Geometria. Geometric "Grammateian" principles were applied by sages called Kabbalists, in their search for the principles, the laws, that are operative in the evolution of life, in the structure, the Building of this our Universe. The proper use of this geometric-grammateian principle furnished to these Hebrew-Jewish-Israelitish sages and theologians, the key to the hidden, the fourfold meaning, of what is today known as the Old Testament.

The Jewish Encyclopedia gives us a very learned treatise on the subject of Gematria, six long pages in reduced type, a great part in the Hebrew-Aramaic- Neo-Hebrew language. The writer of this article in the Jewish Encyclopedia is a great scholar, a modern "Intellectual," therefore a little skeptical. We will give a few quotations:

> *"In Cabalistic literature the use of Gematria has been greatly extended and its forms have been developed in many directions. The principles on which the Gematria rests is not stated in traditional literature, but it may be assumed is essentially the same as that which is found in the Cabala, though in the latter it has been developed along the lines of cosmogonic theories.*
>
> *"A theoretic basis: all creation has developed through emanation from the Ein Sof (Ein Sof is an important Masonic emblem or symbol). The first degrees of that evolution are the ten Sephiroth; from the last of which, the "Kingdom" developed the twenty-two letters of the Hebrew alphabet. Through the latter the whole finite world has come into existence. These letters are dynamic powers. Since these powers are numbers, everything that has sprung from them is number. Number is the essence of things, whose local and temporal relations ultimately depends on numerical proportion.*
>
> *"Everything has its prototype in the world of spirits, that spiritual prototype being the term from which the thing has been developed. As the Essence of things is numbers, the identity of things in numbers demonstrates their identity in essence, etc., etc., etc."*

The writer here wishes to call attention to a few articles recently published in *The Builder*, a "Scientific Masonic Magazine." These articles, entitled "The Essenes," "The Kabala" and "Freemasonry and the Kabala," will also give this information: the nomenclature, the symbolism used, employed, pronounced in Freemasonry is Kabalistic, that is, is taken, borrowed from the Kabbalah. The progenitors of this Kabbalah were an Order, called in history, the Essenes. The self-designation of the members of this Order was Banaim, which word translated into English means "Mason" or "Builder." The aim of every member was to become Rab-Bana, that is a Master Builder.

Albert Pike, the only American Master-Builder to whom the Order of Free and Accepted Masons has erected a monument, and this in the city of Washington, has built his literary structure upon the doctrines of these Kabbalistic Banaim, and on page 202 of his book calls particular attention to these Rab-Banaim, Master-Builders, and he emphasizes the fact that the Kabbalah furnishes to Masonry secrets and symbols.

Modern historians, and even some novelists, claim these Essene Banaims to have been the founders, the pioneers, the propagandists of Christianity. A use of Gematria is recognized by the true Initiate in many pages of the Old and New Testaments. The Jewish Encyclopedia here points to (1) Genesis XIV, 14, where the number 318 is the equivalent of "Eliezer" (2) Deut. XXXII, 1-6 where the initial letters of the verse give the number of 345, equal to the value of the name of Moses and (3) Ezekiel V, 2, where the number 390 is featured.

An instructive illustration or exemplification of Gematria is furnished by "Christian" Kabbalists. The form here prescribed and the principles involved are, or should be, of special interest to members of an organization known by the name of "Modern Freemasonry." These Christian Kabbalists, of whom the church fathers, Clement and Origen, are the most illustrious and best known representatives, were potent factors in the formation of Christian theology, and the propaganda of the Christian faith.

Christian Kabbalists made a special use of the words IOANNES (John) and IESOUS (Jesus) and BAPTISMA was also used. This may be exemplified by a quotation from a book recently published by two unrecognized modern British students of Gematria, Frederic Bligh Bond, F.R.I.B.A., and Thomas S. Lea, D.D.

Here then is a case in which the Gematria value of the spelling might be looked to for light, if our theory be correct, and it must be admitted that the name IOANES has an undeniable importance in view of its divine origin in the gospel narrative. The numerical value of IOANES (Joanes) is 1069, a number not apparently related to the general scheme of mystic numbers which subsists in the writings, but as IOANNES the form generally formed and employed by the old Scribes and which is also to be seen in the Cosmic MS. of the Pistis Sophia, it is 1119, and this it may at once be said, is an important number in the mystical geometry of the Aeons, and is actually the number of the first.

Aeon in the *Books of IEOU* is directly connected with the number 634. The French author, Honore de Balzac, in *Louis Lambert* and *Seraphita,* proclaims a philosophical theology in striking accord with the teaching of the Kabbalah. In this work he presents a world, ideas and doctrines, in striking agreement with the teachings given in and by Gematria. On one page, this French genius enumerates laws and principles that are stated in nearly the same words as are in the Zohar (the Crown of Kabbalah). The following are some of these laws:

"Everything in this world exists only by movement and by number.

"Movement is in some sort, number in action.

"Movement is the product of a force engendered by the word and by a resistances which is matter. Without the resistance, movement would be without result, its action would have been infinitely small. The attraction of Newton is not a law, but an effect of the general law of universal movement."

This is a kind of "Einsteinian" relativity proclaimed in 1835.

Now, Gematria is old, very old. But, dear reader, so is the so-called Atomic theory, so is the miscalled Copernican system of astronomy. Not only had Pythagoras and Plato taught this so-called Copernican or Heliocentric theory, but it was also taught by the Essene Banaims and had been discovered through the modus operandi and quaerendi, called Gematria. This "Heliocentric" doctrine, with Pythagoras and

Plato as well as the Essenes, was of course one of their "Masonic" secrets.

Our friend Albert Pike, in his great work, presents us in the final chapters headed "Knight of the Sun, Prince Adept, and Sublime Prince of the Royal Secret," the most brilliant exhibition and illustration of the modus operandi and opus quaerendi of his friends the Kabbalists. The modus and opus operandi is, as we found out, called Gematria.

Our friend Albert Pike strongly emphasizes the fact that Graeco-Roman sages had employed the same, or similar, modus and opus. Now the question might arise whether the Kabbalist Banaim had borrowed doctrines and ideas from the Pythagorian adepts or Eleusinian Mystics or vice versa. This question has been debated, we will leave it here undecided. In our opinion, no borrowing was necessary. *Veritas habetur clara eternaque.* Seeing at all times depends upon the eyes of the seer.

When the human race is ready for the reception of an idea it is precipitated upon terra firma by the Higher Powers. Again and again a new idea comes to, a new discovery is made by several individuals at the same time; in evolution we have Darwin and Wallace, in mathematics, in calculus, Newton and Leibnitz.

The great Masonic authority, Albert Pike, thinks that Pythagoras had his instruction in Judea from Daniel and Ezekiel. This writer does not endorse this particular opinion of Albert Pike.

Now, son of man, remember the declaration ascribed to King Solomon, "there is nothing new under the sun." One might see a kind of contradiction in this Solomonian proverb in the scientific dictum "nature never repeats." But to this scientific dictum should be added the word "exactly." No two things are exactly alike. So that every human voice even has its own peculiar flavor.

The reader has now been told a lot about ancient Gematria; he might have heard of strange Pythagorean, hermetic, mathematical, astrological superstitions, and now, lo and behold, here comes a great, a recognized, modern scholar and scientist, a Doctor, a Professor at the University of Tubingen. He wrote for the March number of the Preussische Jahrbucher, a conservative German Scientific magazine, a long article entitled "Mathematik und Kultur." Our professor had presumably never studied the Kabbalah; had probably never heard the word Gematria; yet in his article he tells us of some new, strangely mystical, German discovery in the realm of mathematics; discoveries which remind the initiate of doctrines, of ideas and ideals found in the Gematria. Our professor informs us that these strangely mystical "new" discoveries have been found useful not only in theoretical science, but are utilized today in the pursuits of modern industry, such as chemistry, radio- activity and so on.

In this article our learned professor endeavors to place upon a scientific basis, occult teachings about mathematics, the mystical potency of number, in the unfoldment, the manifestation of life in this, our universe.

As these new doctrines are presented in eight printed pages we can give here a few quotations only. Among many other things Dr. Knapp tells us:

"The Pythagoreans succeeded in making a discovery of far reaching significance; they ascertained the laws of Harmony in sound and were able to place these laws upon a Numerical Theoretical Foundation."

That is, Gematria. He theorizes in many words about the importance of this discovery, about the intimate connection, the complementary features possessed by two seemingly heterogeneous elements: Mathematics and Music. Our professor writes:

"The Pythagorean school endeavors to make number, or, more clearly expressed, the relation of numbers, the innermost basis of life and nature.

"Alongside the Harmony of sound, the Pythagorean affirmed with keen speculation the harmony of the spheres, i.e., the doctrine that in the complementary motions of sun, moon and planets there is operative the principle of Numerical potency or power, which law or power resembles, is identical with, the law or power operative in the law of sound. This law in a way is "twin" and becomes affective and effective in the life of men."

Again Professor Knapp says:

"Now I wish to declare that this discovery of the Pythagoreans has found, has experienced a resurrection, a most potent revival in most instances, in the different races. Such as the modern "Quantum

Theory." Here we learn that relation between numbers furnishes for man the mirror in which he finds the unfoldment of Life."

Yet further we find the following:

"The study, the investigation by the ancient Greeks of the Kegelschnitten [i. e., the analysis of the principles involved in the formation of the circle, the eclipse, the parabola and hyperbola] presents a highly interesting field of investigation. Apollonius of Perga gave to this mathematical study his whole lifetime, and we have from him an elaborate presentation of his results in eight books. Some inductions and deductions had seemed strange and mystical. But a few thousands of years later Kepler discovered that planets and comets in their evolution around the sun move in courses indicated and designated in this Kepelschnitten so that what had seemed mathematical playfulness or tomfoolery had the most surprising cosmic significance."

And still further we read:

"Let us return to our Pythagoreans; their Einsichten, their recognitions and the hope of new discoveries gave their study of mathematics a value superior to all other occupations. The Structure, the nature of the Cosmos, was recognized as having a mathematical basis. They did not postulate this mathematical basis for the realm of exteriors, the phenomenal world, alone. For in their judgment the sense of Harmony enters deeply the interior, the human sphere, and thus they made mathematics the basis of all knowledge. We do not know what definite knowledge was reached, what discoveries in the realm of science was made by the Pythagoreans. One thing we do know: they utilized as a fact, or rather as a factor, the potency of numbers. They taught that

number, whole number, was at the beginning, was in a way the Source of the evolution of Life in the bosom of Nature and that the relation between numbers furnished for man the mirror in which he could see the unfoldment of life."

And yet again he says:

"At yet another point in modern progress do we see the potency of the "whole number." I wish here to call attention to the principle of periodicity in the realm of chemical elements, to the fact that every element has a definite whole number, order-of-and-for-process, which order determines so completely the character, the nature of the elements that Max Born, a recognized authority, maintained that the theory of physics and chemistry will become a problem of numbers."

Professor Knapp is here in accord with a statement made by Lord Kelvin in his last visit to this country when speaking to the student body at Cornell University. In this speech he remarked *"The great work of the twentieth century will be in the reconciliation of the life seen with the life unseen, by means of psychophysics."* To this recognition are due some commercially important discoveries in the German chemical industry.

One more quotation we will make from our professor:

"An uneducated individual will not be able to imagine a non-Euclidian geometry, that is a geometry in which matter such as the three angles of a triangle make not 180 degrees, and yet Gauss, and especially Rieman, had posited, had worked with, these non-Euclidian principles. And we know today that the Theory of

Relativity postulated by Einstein is based upon this non-Euclidian geometry.

"Again in Greek history we find that mathematics was revered as the Queen of Science. And now we might say here a few swords about the relation of mathematics to the principle of Philosophy."

Here our professor gives a dissertation too lengthy for a presentation in this sketch.

These declarations are strange, very strange when made by a modern scholar. Our scientists have always looked, and the majority of them today still look askance, at the sphere of the spiritual, the mystical; in other words, the realm of Religion. The claims of the theologians were smiled at, were deemed beneath the honor of an investigation by a real scientist and now the great Gauss is quoted by our professor as saying:

"But all search, every effort was in vain; finally a few days ago there came success; the success was not due to my efforts, my struggle, my powers. Success came like unto a flash of lightning; the problem was solved through the Grace of God."

Now what is the purpose of Gematria? Gematria furnishes a solution for three problems.

1. Gematria teaches the nature of the Cosmos, the origin of this, our Solar System.

2. Gematria teaches the Nature, the Purpose, the Destiny of man, the Genus Homo.

3. Gematria shows to the personality the road on which the wanderer can and eventually must reach, his destination.

The new philosophy has coined a new term, supra-liminal consciousness, and we would like to refer the American reader to the father of psycho- physics, Theodore Fechner. The question of course comes up, what is this supra-liminal consciousness? The phenomena so long rejected by scientists, such as clairvoyance, clairaudience or telepathy, are today "explained" as manifestations of this "supra- consciousness." The scientists would find useful information for the solution of these problems in the study of an occult treatise called the Kabbalah and considered by some as divinely revealed; and in a certain modus operandi designated by the letter G and called Gematria.

Kabbalah and the Origin of Freemasonry

By Eliphas Levi

That great Kabbalistical association known in Europe under the name of Masonry appeared suddenly in the world when revolt against the Church had just succeeded in dismembering Christian unity. The historians of the Order are one and all in a difficulty when seeking to explain its origin. According to some, it derived from a certain guild of Masons who were incorporated for the construction of the cathedral of Strasburg. Others refer its foundation to Cromwell, without pausing to consider whether the Rites of English Masonry in the days of the Protector were not more probably developed as a counter-blast to this leader of Puritanical anarchy. In fine, some are so ignorant that they attribute to the Jesuits the maintenance and direction, if not indeed the invention, of a society long preserved in secret and always wrapped in mystery. Setting aside this last view, which refutes itself, we can reconcile the others by admitting that the Masonic Brethren borrowed their name and some emblems of their art from the builders of Strasburg cathedral, and that their first public manifestation took place in England, owing to radical institutions and in spite of Cromwell's despotism. It may be added that the Templars were their models, the Rosicrucians their immediate progenitors, and the Johannite sectarians their more remote ancestors. Their doctrine is that of Zoroaster and of Hermes, their law is progressive initiation, their principle is equality--

regulated by the hierarchy and universal fraternity. They are successors of the school of Alexandria, as of all antique initiations, custodians of the secrets of the Apocalypse and the Zohar, Truth is the object of their worship, and they represent truth as light; they tolerate all forms of faith, profess one philosophy, seek truth only, teach reality, and their plan is to lead all human intelligence by gradual steps into the domain of reason. The allegorical end of Freemasonry is the rebuilding of Solomon's Temple; the real end is the restoration of social unity by an alliance between reason and faith and by reverting to the principle of the hierarchy, based on science and virtue, the path of initiation and its ordeals serving as steps of ascent. Nothing, it will be seen, is more beautiful, nothing greater than are such ideas and dedications; unhappily the doctrines of unity and submission to the hierarchy have not been maintained in universal Masonry. In addition to that which was orthodox there arose a dissident Masonry, and all that is worst in the calamities of the French Revolution were the result of this schism.

Now, the Freemasons have their sacred legend, which is that of Hiram, completed by another concerning Cyrus and Zerubbabel. The legend of Hiram is as follows. When Solomon projected his Temple, he entrusted the plans to an architect called Hiram. This master-builder, to ensure order in the work, divided the craftsmen according to their degrees of skill. They were a great multitude, and in order to recognize craftsmen, so that they might be classified according to merit or remunerated in proportion to their work, he provided Pass-Words and particular Signs for each of three categories, or otherwise for the Apprentices, the Companions and the Masters. It came about that three Companions coveted the rank of Master without having earned it by their ability. They set an ambush at the three chief gates of the Temple, and when Hiram was issuing from one of them, the first of these Companions demanded the Master-Word, threatening the architect with his rule. Hiram answered: "It is not thus that I received it." Thereupon the Companion in his fury struck him with the iron tool and gave him the first wound. The builder fled to the second gate, where he met with the second Companion, who made the same demand and received the same answer. On this occasion Hiram was struck with a square or, as others say, with a lever. At the third gate there stood the third assassin, who completed the work with a mallet. The three companions concealed the corpse under a heap of rubbish, planted on the improvised grave a branch of acacia, and then took flight like Cain after the murder of Abel. Solomon, however, finding that his architect did not return, sent nine Masters to seek him, when the branch of acacia revealed the corpse. They drew it from beneath the rubbish, and as it had laid long therein, they uttered in so doing a word signifying that the flesh was falling from the bones. The last offices were rendered duly to Hiram, and twenty-seven Masters were dispatched subsequently by Solomon in search of the murderers. The first of these was taken by surprise in a cavern; a lamp was burning near him, a stream flowed at his feet and a dagger lay for his defense beside him. The Master who had been first to enter recognized the assassin, seized the weapon and stabbed him with the exclamation Nekam a word signifying vengeance. The head was carried to Solomon, who shuddered at the sight and said to the avenger: "Unhappy being, did you not know that I reserved to myself the right of punishment?" Then all the Masters fell on their knees before the king and entreated pardon for him whose zeal had carried him away. The second murderer was betrayed by one with whom he had found an asylum. He was concealed in a rock near to a burning bush; a rainbow shone above the rock, and a dog lay near him. Eluding the vigilance of the dog, the Masters seized the criminal, bound and carried him to Jerusalem, where he perished in the utmost tortures. The third assassin was slain by a lion, and the beast had to be overcome before the body could be secured. Other versions say that he defended himself with a hatchet when the Masters fell upon him, but they succeeded in disarming him and he was led to Solomon who caused him to expiate his crime.

Such is the first legend and its explanation now follows. Solomon personifies supreme science and wisdom. The Temple is the realization and emblem of the hierarchic reign of truth and reason on earth. Hiram is the man who, by science and wisdom, has attained empire. He governs by justice and order, rendering to each according to his works. Each Degree is in correspondence with a word, which expresses the sense thereof. For Hiram the word is one, but it is expressed after three manners. One is for the Apprentices and can be uttered by them; it signifies Nature and is explained by Work. Another is for the Companions; in their case it signifies thought and is explained by Study. The third is for Masters; in their mouth it signifies truth and is explained by Wisdom. As to the word itself, it is used to designate God, whose true name is indicible and incommunicable. Thus, there are three degrees in the hierarchy and three entrances of the Temple; there are three modes of light and there are three forces in Nature, which forces are symbolized by the Rule that measures, the Lever which lifts and the Mallet which consolidates. The rebellion of brutal instincts against the hierarchic aristocracy of wisdom arms itself successfully with these three forces and turns them from their proper uses. There are three typical rebels - the rebel against Nature, the rebel against Science and the rebel against Truth. They were represented in the classical Hades by the three heads of Cerberus; in the Bible by Korah, Dathan and Abiram; while in the Masonic legend they are distinguished by names which vary in the different Rites. The first, who is usually called Abiram, or the murderer of Hiram, is he who strikes the Grand Master with the rule; this is the story of the just man immolated by human passion under the pretense of law. The second, named Mephibosheth, after a ridiculous and feeble pretender to the throne of David, attacks Hiram with the lever or the square. So does the popular square or lever of insensate equality become an instrument of tyranny in the hands of the multitude, and assails, still more grievously than the rule, the royalty of wisdom and virtue. The third in fine dispatches Hiram with a mallet: so act the brutal instincts when they seek to establish order, in the name of violence and of fear, by crushing intelligence.

The branch of acacia over the tomb of Hiram is like the cross on our altars; it is a sign of knowledge which outlives knowledge itself; it is the green sprig which presages another spring. When men have disturbed in this manner the order of Nature, Providence intervenes to restore it, as Solomon to avenge the death of the Master-Builder. He who has struck with the rule shall perish by the poignard. He who as attacked with the lever or square shall make expiation under the axe of the law: it is the eternal judgment on regicides. He who has slain with the mallet shall be the victim of that power which he misused. He who would slay with the rule is betrayed by the very lamp which lights him and by the stream from which he drinks: it is the law of retaliation. He who would destroy with the lever is surprised when his watchfulness fails like a sleeping dog, and he is given up by his own accomplices, for anarchy is the mother of treason. He who struck with the mallet is devoured by the lion, which is a variant of the sphinx of Oedipus, while he who can conquer the lion shall deserve to succeed Hiram. The decaying body of the Builder indicates that forms may change but the spirit remains. The spring of water in the vicinity of the first murderer recalls that deluge which punished crimes against Nature. The burning bush and rainbow which betray the second assassin typify life and light denouncing outrage on thought. Finally, the vanquished lion represents the triumph of mind over matter and the definite subjection of force to intelligence. From the dawn of the intellectual travail by which the Temple of unity is erected, Hiram has been slain often, but ever he has risen from the dead. He is Adonis destroyed by the wild boar, Osiris put to death by Typhon, Pythagoras in his proscription, Orpheus torn to pieces by Bacchantes, Moses abandoned in the caverns of Mount Nebo, Jesus crucified by Judas, Caiaphas and Pilate. Now those are true Masons who seek persistently to rebuild the Temple in accordance with the plan of Hiram.

Such is the great and the chief legend of Masonry there are others that are no less beautiful and no less profound; but we do not feel justified in divulging their mysteries. Albeit we have received initiation only from God and our researches, we shall keep the secrets of transcendental Freemasonry as we keep our own secrets. Having attained by our efforts to a grade of knowledge, which imposes silence, we regard ourselves as pledged by our convictions even more than by an oath. Science is a *noblesse qui oblige* and we shall in no wise fail to deserve the princely crown of the Rosy Cross. We also believe in the resurrection of Hiram.

The Rites of Masonry are designed to transmit a memorial of the legends of initiation and to preserve them among the Brethren. Now, if Masonry is thus holy and thus sublime, we may be asked how it came to be proscribed and condemned so often by the Church; but we have already replied to this question when its divisions and profanations were mentioned. Masonry is the Gnosis and the false Gnostics caused the condemnation of the true. The latter were driven into concealment, not through fear of the light, for the light is that which they desire, that which they seek and adore; but they stood in dread of the sacrilegious- that is to say, of false interpreters, calumniators, the derision of the skeptic, the enemies of all belief and all morality. Moreover, at the present day, there are many who think that they are Masons and yet do not know the meaning of their Rites, having lost the Key of the Mysteries. They misconstrue even their symbolical pictures and those hieroglyphic signs which are emblazoned on the carpets of their Lodges. These pictures and signs are the pages of a book of absolute and universal science. They can be read by means of the Kabalistic keys and hold nothing in concealment for the initiate who already possesses those of Solomon.

Masonry has not merely been profaned but has served as the veil and pretext of anarchic conspiracies depending from the secret influence of the vindicators of Jacques de Molay, and of those who continued the schismatic work of the Temple. In place of avenging the death of Hiram they have avenged that of his assassins. The anarchists have resumed the rule, square and mallet, writing upon them the words Liberty, Equality, Fraternity --Liberty, that is to say, for all the lusts, Equality in degradation and Fraternity in the work of destruction. Such are the men whom the Church has condemned justly and will condemn forever.

Notes on the Kabbalah of the Old Testament

By J. Ralston Skinner

In a previous article on Hebrew Metrology, I said that the system embracing it was a language, veiled under the Hebrew text of Scripture, and that *"To the extent of which the language was known among the Jews, the learning and teaching thereof was called the Kabbalah."*

It is a fact that, so little is known of the Kabbalah, that its existence has been denied. It has seemed to possess a like property with that of *Prester John*. Namely, the more and further he was searched for, the less he could be found and the more fabulous he became. After the same fashion, as very much was related of wonders connected with *Prester John*, so are the most marvelous things claimed for Kabbalah. The Kabbalistic field is that in which astrologers, necromancers, black and white magicians, fortunetellers, chiromancers, and all the like, revel and make claims to supernaturalism *ad nauseam*. Claim is also made that it conceals a sublime divine philosophy, which has been attempted to be set forth in a most confused and not understandable way. The Christian who quarries into this mass of mysticism, claims for their support and authority of that most perplexing of all problems, the Holy Trinity, and the betrayed character of Christ. The good, pious and ignorant man picks up Kabbalah at will, as a cheap, easy and veritable production, and at once, with the poorest smattering of starved ideas, gives forth to the world, as by authority, a devout jumble of stuff and nonsense. With equal insurance, but more effrontery, the knave, in the name of the Kabbalah, will sell amulets and charms, tell fortunes, draw horoscopes, and just as readily give specific rules, as in the case of the worthy Dr. John Dee, for raising the dead, and actually — the devil.

No wonder then that the whole affair has been discredited and condemned by the rational and the wise.

Discovery has yet to be made of what the Kabbalah really consists of, before any weight or authority can be given to the name. On that discovery will rest the question as to whether the name should be received as related to matters worthy of rational acknowledgment.

The writer claims that such a discovery *has* been made, and that the same embraces rational and sober science of great worth. He claims that it will serve to clear up and take away very much of the mysticism which up to this time has been an unexplainable part of religious systems, — especially the Hebrew or Jewish, and the Christian, so much so that the supernatural in those systems will have to give place to the rational, to a very great extent. He claims that the sublime science, upon which Masonry is based, is in fact, the substance of the Kabbalah — which last is the rational basis of the Hebrew text of Holy writ.

Kabbalah is inseparably connected with the text of the Scriptures, and an exposition of the inner sense of the same is as John Reuchlin claimed necessary to a right and full understanding of the Sacred Text. But he saw vaguely, being taught only in a mystic phraseology which was really a blind, and he did not come into possession of the solid, rational grounds of it which he could formulate and impart. For this reason, though he was right in his general assertion, his scheme failed, and his works in this regard, passed away from the common sense world, and have ever since lived only among the mystics and dreamers.

Like all other human productions of the kind, the Hebrew text of the Bible was in characters which could serve as sound signs for syllabic utterance, or for this purpose what are called letters. Now in the first place, these original character signs were also pictures, each one of them; and these pictures of themselves stood for ideas which could be communicated, — much like the original Chinese letters. Gustav Seyffarth shows that the Egyptian hieroglyphics numbered over six hundred picture characters, which embraced the modified use, syllabically, of the original number of letters of the Hebrew alphabet. The characters of the Hebrew text of the Sacred Scroll were divided into classes, in which the characters of each class were interchangeable; whereby one form might be exchanged for another to carry a modified signification, both by letter, and picture and number. Seyffarth shows the modified form of the very ancient Hebrew alphabet in the old Coptic by this law of interchange of characters. This law of permitted interchange of letters is to be found quite fully set forth in the Hebrew dictionaries, such as Fuerst's and others. Though recognized and largely set forth it is very perplexing and hard to understand, because we have lost the specific use and power of such interchange. In the second place, these characters stood for numbers — to be used for numbers as we use specific number signs, — though, also, there is very much to prove that the old Hebrews were in possession of the so-called Arabic numerals, as we have them, from the straight line 1 to the zero character, together making 1+9=10. The order of these number letters run from 1 to 9, then 10 to 90, then 100 upward. In the third place it is said, and it seems to be proven, that these characters stood for musical notes; so that for instance, the arrangement of the letters in the first chapter of Genesis, can be rendered musically, or by song. Another law of the Hebrew characters was that only the consonantal signs were characterized, — the vowels were not characterized, but were supplied. If one will try he will find that a consonant of itself cannot be made vocal without the help of a vowel; therefore it was said that the consonants made the frame work of a word, but to give it life or utterance into the air, so as to impart the thought of the mind, and the feeling of the heart, the vowels had to be supplied. Thus the dead word of consonants became quickened into life by the Holy Spirit, or the vowels.

This being said then: —

First: The Holy or Sacred Text was given in consonants only, without any voweling, or signs of vowels.

Second: The letters were written one after the other at equal distances, without any separation whatever of distinct words, and without any punctuations whatever, such as commas, semi-colons, colons or periods.

It will be seen at once that a various reading of the text might be had in many places, both by differing arrangements of letters, and by a differing supplying of vowels. A very important difference of reading may be instanced in the first line of Genesis. It is made to be read "B'rashith bara Elohim," etc., "In the beginning God created the heavens and the earth"; wherein Elohim is a plural nominative to a verb in the third person singular. Nahmanides called attention to the fact that the text might suffer the reading, "B'rash ithbara Elohim," etc. "In the head (source or beginning) created itself (or developed) Gods, the heavens and the earth," — really a more grammatical rendering.

What the originally and intended right reading was who can tell? It may be surmised, however, that it was made to subserve a coordinating, symmetrical and harmonious working of the characters to unfold and develop their various uses; — as sound signs to frame a narrative, — as numbers to develop geometrical shapes and the numerical enunciations of their elements, comparisons and applications, — as pictures to show forth ideas in some accordance with the story told, and finally, — as musical sounds to give an appropriate song to embrace the whole. The whole compass was to embrace rational proof, through operations in nature, of the existence of that Divine Contriving Willing Cause which we call God. But be this as it may there was no end of effort for thousands of years, by the best trained and most learned men of the Hebrews and Jews, to give and preserve what had to be decided upon by them as the right reading of the Sacred Text. This reading was certainly perfected as we have it, as early as the time of Ezra; and as to the various readings which offered, the present was perfected as the orthodox one, — or that one to be received by the profound vulgar.

It must be known that it is claimed for the Sacred Scroll by the Hebrew, that no letter in it has ever been changed, and that even the marginal readings were part of the original text for a varied use thereof, in perfect accord with the object of its writing. Unlike the Christian Gospels, with the Hebrews and Jews, alike, the original text was sacredly precious as to its every and very letter, and had to be thus preserved. To the contrary of this, the Gospels can be changed in their reading to suit the currently changing ideas of what the same should be. The marks to indicate "right reading" were after the time of Ezra gradually made public, were called Masorah, and finally, edited by Jakob ben Chajim, were published by Bomberg, in Venice, in the fifteenth century.

After this fashion and mode the books of the Old Testament were prepared and read by the Jews long before the time of the Christian Era. They were thus accepted at that time; and afterwards by the Christian World: — so that, today, we accept the record, as thus prepared by the ancient orthodox Jewish and Hebrew Church.

Whatever may have been the Jewish mode of complete interpretation of these books, the Christian Church had taken them for what they show on their first face, — and that only. As they may be read orally, so is their fullest meaning to be gathered from the oral reading; and by means of what the sound of the words may convey to the ear the full and complete intendment of meaning is to be had. The Christian Church has never attributed to these books any property beyond this; and herein has existed its great error.

Now, as said, the substance of the Kabbalah is a rendering of the secret doctrine of the Old Testament, and this is not only asserted, but an argument is raised about the matter in the following set terms: "If the Law simply consisted of ordinary expressions and narratives, ex. gr. the words of Esau, Hagar, Laban, the ass of Balaam, or of Balaam himself, why should it be called the Law of Truth, the perfect law, the true witness of God? Each word contains a sublime source, each narrative points not only to the single instance in question, but also to generals." (*Zohar* iii, 149 b). "Woe be to the son of man who says that the Tora (Pentateuch) contains common sayings and ordinary narratives. "There is the garment that everyone can see, but those who have more understanding do not look at the garment but at the body beneath it; while the wisest, the servants of the Heavenly King, those who dwell at Mount Sinai, look at nothing else but the soul (i.e., the secret doctrine), which is the root of all the real Law." (*Zohar*, iii, 152 a).

Now it is a strange thing, that in the quotations made by Dr. Ginsburg in his Essay (*The Kabbalah, its Doctrine, Development and Literature*), can be gleaned a series of data wherewith to arrange a philosophy of Cabbalistic teaching, covered by the names and remarks on the Ten Sephiroth. The "trick of the thing" lays plainly before the eyes in its development, and yet is perfectly concealed from unintelligent observation. In other words, the very text is laughing at the worthy doctor, while he is criticizing it with an apparent aspect of superiority and authority. The same thing is to be found in the text of Plutarch's Morals, by C. W. King, and in many other texts where the like phenomenal mode is practiced. It in fact is said that the Kabbalah is evolved by "hints scarcely perceptible," and the cunning of the concealment is something to admire and laugh at. The description in *Zohar* of the mode of communication tends to explain what has been said:

> "The opinion that the mysteries of the Kabbalah are to be found in the garment of the Pentateuch is still more systematically propounded in the following parable: 'Like a beautiful woman, concealed in the interior of her palace, who when her friend and beloved passes by, opens for a moment a secret window and is seen by him alone, and then withdraws herself immediately and disappears for a long time, so the doctrine only shows herself to the chosen (i.e., to him who is devoted to her with body and soul); and even to him not always in the same manner. At first she simply beckons at the passer by with her hand, and it generally depends upon his understanding this gentle hint. This is the interpretation known by the name of ramaz. Afterwards she approaches him a little closer, lisps him a few words but her form is still covered with a thick veil, which his looks cannot penetrate. This is the so-called darausch. She

then converses with him with her face covered by a thin veil; this is the enigmatic language of the hagadah. After having thus become accustomed to her society, she at last shows herself face to face and entrusts him with the innermost secrets of her heart. This is the secret of the Law, sod. He who is thus far initiated in the mysteries of the Tora will understand that all these profound secrets are based upon the simple literal sense, and are in harmony with it, and from this literal sense not a single iota is to be taken and nothing is to be added to it." (*Zohar*, ii, 99.)

Ginsburg and others tell us that Raymond Lully and Giovanni Pico della Mirandola had acquired knowledge of the Hebrew and the Kabbalah. Mirandola studied Hebrew and Cabbalistic theology under Jochanan Aleman, who came to Italy from Constantinople, and — "found that there is more Christianity in the Kabbalah than Judaism; he discovered in it proof for the doctrine of the Trinity, the Incarnation, the Divinity of Christ, the heavenly Jerusalem, the fall of the angels, the order of the angels" and so on, and so on. "In 1486, when only 24 years old, he published 900 theses, which were placarded in Rome, and which he undertook to defend in the presence of all European scholars, whom he invited to the Eternal City, promising to defray their traveling expenses. Among the theses was the following: 'No science yields greater proof of the Divinity of Christ than magic and the Kabbalah.'"

Through Pico della Mirandola, Reuchlin became aware of this phase of Hebrew philosophy or theosophy, as, by a school of the rabbins, a recognized appurtenant to the Hebrew Scriptures. He not only examined into the Kabbalah to satisfy his thirst for facts of literature, but on investigation became a convert to the system, — "within two years of beginning to learn the language, published (1494) his *De Verbo Mirifico*, and afterwards (1516) with more matured learning, his *De Arte Cabalistica*." And thus the joint efforts of Mirandola and Reuchlin established a field of literature, of the Kabbalah, which has always flourished, and will continue to flourish so long as our civilization shall last.

It is interesting and useful to place this great fact, but it is a matter of especially great weight and value that the knowledge of the Kabbalah was sprung upon the world of letters, with, and as an essential part of the Reformation itself. Not that the philosophy of the Kabbalah became engrafted into the study and development of Hebrew (and consequently Christian) theosophy; — for, because of lack of knowledge of what the Kabbalah really was, such could not be the case, — but it was entitled so to be, and the assertion of its existence as a real element of Scripture was, even then, so strongly and enduringly made, that, though an unknown quantity except by name, it has ever since stood firmly, and ready to have such claim made good: — with a vitality that has outworn four hundred years of patient waiting.

Of course there was a field of Jewish Cabbalistic literature, — not open, but confined, for the most part, as a kind of sacred mystery, within narrow and restricted limits, even among the Jews themselves. It was of the same nature with what is called, today, The Speculative Philosophy of Freemasonry, an ever seemingly substantive embodiment out of surrounding shadowy mists and mental logs, wherein a doubt always exists whether after all there is in the nebulous matter of the mist itself anything from whence substance may congeal: or, it may, for illustration, be compared to the city of King Arthur, before whose gate Gareth, standing, says: "But these my men — (your city moves so weirdly in the mist), — doubt if the King be King at all, or come from Fairy land: and whether this be built by magic, and by fury kings and queens, or whether there be any city at all, or all a vision." It is necessary to make a brief mention of this literature with its sources: both that these may be known, and that a foundation may be laid for what is stated as to the reality of Kabbalah, and its significance.

There is almost no teaching of the Kabbalah in the English language except the Essay by Christian D. Ginsburg, to which we have referred. Dr. Ginsburg says: "It is a system of religious philosophy, or more properly, of theosophy, which has not only exercised for hundreds of years are extraordinary influence on the mental development of so shrewd a people as the Jews, but has captivated the minds of some of the greatest thinkers of Christendom in the sixteenth and seventeenth centuries, and which claims the greatest attention of both the philosopher and theologian."

It is faintly claimed that some statements applying to Kabbalah are to be found in the Talmud; but apart from this we have: — (1) The Commentary on the Ten Sephiroth, by R. Azariel ben Menachem (1160 - 1238), who was a pupil of Isaac the Blind, and master of the celebrated R. Moses Nahmanides, (2) The *Zohar* (Light), or Midrash, Let there be Light, claimed to have been a revelation from God, communicated through R. Simeon ben Yochai, A.D. 70-110, to his select disciples. This book has been pronounced by the ablest critics to have been a pseudograph of the thirteenth century, — the composition of Moses de Leon, who lived in Spain; who, by the admission of his wife and daughter after his death, first published and sold it as the production of R. Simeon ben Yochai, and (3) The *Sepher Yetzirah* or Book of Creation, — of unknown age and authorship, and mentioned as early as the eleventh century in the Kitab al Khazari, by R. Judah Halevi, — as the literary sources for the entire system and scope thereof, so far as disclosed, it is from these sources that the entire volume of Cabbalistic literature has had rise and development.

From these sources, and the numberless treatises and expositions thereon, the history of the subject matter and containment of Kabbalah is laid down as follows: It was first taught by God himself to a select company of angels. After the fall the angels taught it to Adam. From Adam it passed to Noah, thence to Abraham, the friend of God who carried it to Egypt. Moses, who was learned in all the wisdom of Egypt, was initiated into it from the land of his birth. He covertly laid down the principles of its doctrines in the first four books of the Pentateuch, but withheld them from Deuteronomy ("this constitutes the former the 'man' and the latter the 'woman'"). Moses initiated the seventy elders, and they again passed the sacred and secret doctrine down to the heads (continually imparting the same) of the Church of Israel. David and

Solomon were adepts in it. No one dared to write it down till the supposititious Simeon ben Yochai, who really lived and taught, as one of the most celebrated doctors, at the time of the destruction of the second temple: and his teachings are claimed to constitute the Book of *Zohar*, published, as already said, by Moses de Leon of Valladolid, in Spain. But ben Yochai, or whoever worked under his name, though he wrote and published, as said, covered the true doctrine by veils, so that no one but an initiate, or, as the saying runs, "by the gift of God" could penetrate behind them; — though the veils of the words still plainly held the secret doctrine, to those who could see. The Kabbalah, as an exposition to the Sacred Text of Holy Writ, was claimed to contain the Wisdom of God in every branch and department of His working, — and all terms and descriptions were exhausted to express the ineffable reward to him who might be permitted to penetrate behind the veil, either by initiation or "by the gift of God;" satiating every function of enjoyment, and affording an indescribable bliss, in the ultimate possessions of the Divine conceptions.

More definitely: — The exposition of the system treats of the impersonal First Cause manifesting within the limits of the finite. "Before he gave any shape to this world, before he produced any form, he was alone, without a form and resemblance to anything else. Who, then, can comprehend him, how he was before the creation, since he was formless? Hence, it is forbidden to represent him by any form, similitude, or even by his sacred name, by a single letter or a single point; and to this, the words, 'Ye saw no manner of similitude on the day the Lord spake unto you' (Deut. iv. 15) — i.e., ye have nor seen anything which you could represent by any form or likeness, — refer" (Zohar 42 b, 43 a, Sec. AB): — And this shows clearly enough that the supposed sacred names of Scripture do not have reference to the Impersonal First Cause, as its essential designations, but rather to its creations. Then — "The creation, or the universe, is simply the garment of God woven from the Deity's own substance (The Impersonal manifesting in the cosmos, in modes to be expressed by the sacred names and otherwise). For although, to reveal himself to us, the Concealed of all the Concealed, sent forth the Ten Emanations (the Ten Sephiroth) called the Form of God, Form of the Heavenly-Man, yet since even this luminous form was too dazzling for our vision, it had to assume another form, or had to put on another garment which consists of the universe. The universe, therefore, or the visible world, is a further expansion of the Divine Substance, and is called in the Kabbalah, 'the Garment of God.'" (Zohar i, 2 a) — "The whole universe, however, was incomplete, and did not receive its finishing stroke till man was formed, who is the acme of the creation, and the macrocosm uniting in himself the totality of beings, — 'the heavenly Adam,' i.e., the Ten Sephiroth, who emanated from the highest primordial obscurity (The Impersonal First Cause), created the earthly Adam" (Zohar ii, 70 b). This is more definitely expressed in another place, where it says: — "Jehovah (for which stands the letter yod, or j or i) descended on Sinai in fire" the word for which is [*Aleph Shin*] fire. Let the j, or i, the signature for Jehovah, descend in the midst of this word, and one will have [*Aleph Yod Shin*], which is the Hebrew word for man; thus man became out of the Divine fire — "Man is both the import and the highest degree of creation, for which reason he was formed on the sixth day. As soon as man was created everything was complete, including the upper and nether world, for everything is comprised in man. He unites in himself all forms." (Zohar iii, 48 a) — "But after he created the form of the Heavenly Man, he used it as a chariot (Mercabah) (wheels, circles) wherein to descend, and wishes to be called by this form, which is the sacred name Jehovah." (Zohar i, 42 b, 43 a, section A B.)

It is to be observed especially, as to the ground work of the Kabbalah, that the first manifestation was in the "Ten Sephiroth" or Emanations, so called, out of which came the "Heavenly Man"; and the human or earth man represented these Ten Sephiroth in himself. "The lower world is made after the pattern of the upper world; everything which exists in the upper world is to be found as it were in a copy on earth; still the whole is one." (Zohar i, 20 a.)

Thus it is that the compass of the Kabbalah, by *Zohar*, is idealized in the form of a man. This man represented the combination of the Ten Sephiroth, or, as systematically called, Emanations, in which as a unity the whole cosmos existed in its segregated detail; and through which all knowledge thereof, physically, psychically and spiritually, was to be had, in passiveness and in activities; — and through which these activities, as of all potencies — as of angels and powers, — had their special existences. These Emanations had names of qualities, as Beauty, Strength, Wisdom, etc., etc., each name being located upon one of nine parts marked out on the form of the man; each of which was called a Sephira. The totality of the man being taken as one, this added to the nine made ten; and as a number this was the letter Yod, already spoken of. The locations of these Sephiroth (shown as circles) are united one with another, so that one Emanation may flow into another; one into all, and all into one; — and the 22 letters of the alphabet with the 10 vowel sounds, are found therein, or thereby; and these are called the "thirty-two ways or paths of Wisdom"; and as these letters stood also for numbers, there is in this containment every possible mode of expression by word and number. The exposition of the Old Testament, especially the Tora, in the secret or esoteric way, is claimed under this statement; — that is, by numbering the letters of words, and by their permutations and changes of positions; so that this is one of the functions of the Emanations or Sephiroth; and a mighty one for disclosing the Wisdom of God.

The *Sepher Yetzirah* deals especially with these letters and numbers: "By thirty-two paths of secret wisdom, the Eternal, the Lord of Hosts, the God of Israel, the living God, the King of the Universe, the Merciful and Gracious, the High and Exalted God, He who inhabiteth eternity, Glorious and Holy is His name, hath created the worldly means of numbers, phonetic language and writing."

The Commentary on the Ten Sephiroth, by R. Azariel ben Menahem, as its name implies, is directly in consonance with the *Zohar*.

As to the *Sepher Yetzirah*, Dr. Ginsburg says: "The Book Yetzirah, which the Cabbalists claim is their oldest document, has really nothing in common with the cardinal doctrines of the Kabbalah. There is not a word in it bearing on the En Soph (Impersonal First Cause), the Archetypal Man," and so on, and so on. But here the doctor is at fault for this reason: — The word "Sephiroth" means "Numbers" and the Ten Sephiroth means the Ten Numbers; and in the Cabbalistic way these are composed out of a geometrical shape. The circle is the first naught, but out of this naught develops a straight vertical line, viz: the diameter of this circle. This is the first One; and having a first one, from it comes 2 and 3 and 4 and 5 and 6 and 7 and 8 and 9, — the circle or naught and its diameter one, the embracement of all together, forming the comprehensive Ten, or Ten Numbers, Ten Sephiroth, Ten Emanations, the Heavenly Wan, the great YAH, of the ineffable name. Hence the contents of the *Sepher Yetzirah* are of the very essence of the other two, and all are one.

www.ingramcontent.com/pod-product-compliance
Lightning Source LLC
LaVergne TN
LVHW041459070426
835507LV00009B/688